NOT-FOR-PROFIT BUSINESS

Eurydice Moore, M.A., PhD

www.mcclurepublishing.com

DISCLAIMER

Dr. Eurydice Moore is not an attorney; therefore, seek legal advice where applicable. The information shared in this book is strictly for educational and informational purpose only. Seek a professional where applicable.

THIS BOOK PROJECT WAS MADE POSSIBLE THROUGH FUNDING BY:

A partnership with the Chicago Housing Authority (CHA) & Housing Urban Development (HUD)'s Section 3 BUSINESS CONCERN COMPETITIVE GRANT

Not-For-Profit Business - Copyright © 2017

All rights reserved. Printed and bound in the United States of America. According to the 1976 United States Copyright Act, no part of this book may be reproduced or utilized in any form or by any means, electronic or mechanical, including photocopying, recording, or by any information storage or retrieval system, except by a reviewer who may quote brief passages in a review to be printed in a magazine or newspaper, without permission in writing from the Publisher: Inquiries should be addressed to McClure Publishing, Inc. Permissions Department, 398 West Army Trail Road, #124, Bloomingdale, Illinois 60108. Publication date: June 30, 2017.

The author and publisher have made every effort to ensure the accuracy and completeness of information contained in this book. We assume no responsibility for errors, inaccuracies, omissions, or any inconsistencies therein.

Any slights of people, places, belief systems or organizations are unintentional. Any resemblance to anyone living, dead or somewhere in between is truly coincidental.

ISBN 13: 978-0-9989223-0-0

Cover Design and Interior Layout by Kathy McClure
https://www.mcclurepublishing.com

Order additional copies, please contact
books@mcclurepublishing.com
800-659-4908

ACKNOWLEDGEMENTS

Anna White

I dedicate this book in memory of my maternal great-grandmother Anna White. She showed me charity by taking me in at three months of age. My great-grandmother was known as Big Mama in the community. She fed people and housed people that were at a disadvantage in life during her generation. Anna even raised other people that were non-related to her. Upon her death, over 3,000 people attended her wake at standing room only. People were out the door at the funeral to pay tribute to my amazement, and many announced she helped them. It is because of her, I have a charitable heart. She was my introduction to charitable work also known as Not-For-Profit. She did not have an official organization, but she had the heart and fortitude to serve. I salute you, Anna.

Doreen Mormans from Mormans Consulting

I dedicate this book to you as well. You bailed me out of a difficult situation and were very instrumental in assisting me to obtain a business grant to update and upgrade my skills so that I would better serve my clients. I will never forget your labor of love.

God

Always and forever!!! It's because of You that I live, move and have my being. You made it all possible to publish four books. This is miraculous. It's divine.

Kathy McClure

I want to thank you for your professionalism and kindness. You have gone above the call of duty. I thank you for your encouragement.

INTRODUCTION

This book is a self-help and step-by-step guide for starting a Not-for-Profit business to assist those individuals who just started out in human services that do not have substantial amounts of money to pay out to lawyers and certified public accountants. The benefits and the uniqueness of the book is that it has a one stop format concept.

This guide keeps you from having to go from one governmental agency to another governmental agency. Everything is in one book and reveals some things that are not shared because each agency is concerned only about their units and do not help you to prepare for the next step. The author shares helpful tips from over thirty (30) years of Not-for-Profit education, work experience from entry level positions, administration, and CEO of two Not-for-Profit organizations. The author has Not-For-Profit experience with schools, churches, agencies, community advocacy, and cultural centers that will assist readers in transitioning into the world of Not-for-Profit.

This is a quick reference guide that will assist individuals that is considering starting a Not-for-Profit organization on a shoestring budget. This book will explore the various types of Not-for-Profits especially those that people are not aware of such as churches, ministries, schools, agencies, civic centers, cultural centers, and multimedia centers. The reader will be able to follow an A-Z checklist from incorporating to obtaining a 501(c)(3) tax-exempt status from the Internal Revenue Service.

This book is for anyone interested in performing charitable acts from starting an after school program, domestic violence counseling, senior housing, etc. This guide will be helpful to those with an education or background in human services, community services, ministers, counselors, therapists, and even college students considering starting their own Not-for-Profit organizations.

Table of Contents

                                                            Page

ACKNOWLEDGEMENTS

INTRODUCTION

NFP Incorporation 13

    I.   The Origin of Not-for-Profit 20

    II.   Types of Not-for-Profit 21

    III.   Name 24

    IV.   Board 24

    V.   Minutes 26

    VI.   Vision Statement 31

    VII. Mission Statement 33

    VIII. Secretary of State 34

    IX.   Articles of Incorporation 34

              A. Corporation Name and Address 35

              B. Registered Agent 37

              C. Registered Agent's Address Qualifications 37

              D. Initial Board Members 38

              E. Project Activities 38

              F. SIGNATURES 39

    X.   CERTIFICATE OF GOOD STANDING 39

    XI.   IN CONCLUSION OF NFP INCORPORATION 40

NFP 501(c)(3) 41

    I.   Why A 501(c)(3) 41

II.	IRS	41
III.	Benefits of 501(c)(3)	44
IV.	Employer Identification Number (EIN)	45
V.	501(c)(3) Application	48
VI.	Bylaws	56
VII.	Fundraising	59
VIII.	Program Narratives	62
IX.	Annual Budget	63
X.	Conflict of Interest	65
XI.	Non-Profit Tax Reporting	65
XII.	Churches/Others	67

NFP OTHER 71

I.	Charitable Policy	71
II.	Attorney General Office	71
III.	The Department of Revenue	72
IV.	Business Registration	73
V.	Business License	73
VI.	Dun & Bradstreet	74
VII.	SAM	74
VIII.	Unrelated Business Activities	75
IX.	Sustainability	76
X.	Collaborative Activities	78
XI.	Liability Insurance	79
XII.	Brochures/Stationery/Business Cards	80
XIII.	Website/Social Media	80

XIV. Payroll 81

XV. Additional Items 82

Additional Acknowledgements

NFP Incorporation

After over thirty (30) years of experience in Nonprofit ("NP") also referred to as Not-For-Profit ("NFP") and Non-Governmental Organizations, this book was written with you in mind. Surprisingly, the majority of my work experience has been associated with some type of NFP.

My first job was a high school student working for the summer in the mayor's youth program. The minimum age to be processed was sixteen (16) years of age. My folks did not have much money after paying off the bills, and I got tired of always wearing my cousin's Debra hand-me-downs year-after-year.

A project which is long gone called Henry Horner in Chicago, Illinois had a social center that contains a library. I was hired as a librarian's assistant and was responsible for re-shelving books and serving as a messenger. Libraries and social centers are considered NFPs. I had no idea that the pathway laid out to me would be where I would spend the majority of my work experience. After that, I attended Lucy Flower High School another NFP organization.

Some schools are NFPs. It was in my sophomore year that my biology teacher Patricia Barto approached me about signing up into a work study program in which she trained young girls in laboratory procedures. The study programed allowed me to receive laboratory instructions in my junior year of high school. In my senior year, I was assigned to a hospital to receive additional training as a paid position. When it came time to graduate, I had a high school diploma with a trade cooperative laboratory program, and had obtained both the education and experience to be employable as a laboratory assistant. It would be up to the hospital to continue to employ me if they so desired.

The hospital in which I received training was Mary Thompson Hospital located on the west side of Chicago. However, prior to my senior year, during the summer, Ms. Barto would send me to the University of Illinois for a summer job to train in the Microbiology Department. In the fall of my senior year, I was sent to Thompson. I remained there two more additional years after my high school graduation, and the pathologist talked me into going to college to obtain a degree and to become a medical laboratory technician. I studied for the state board certification to receive the stamp of approval by the American Society of Clinical Pathologists also known as ASCP which you carried behind your name that you are both certified and registered.

Hospitals are also NFPs. A tender trap was laid for me. Years would pass and I would work at Mount Sinai Hospital, Cook County Hospital, and my last hospital stint was Rush-Presbyterian St. Luke, which has now been renamed Rush Medical Center. I would serve a total of twelve (12) years in the healthcare industry. A door supernaturally opened for me to replace my teacher Ms. Patricia Barto, and I returned to the other side of the desk as both a science teacher and the coordinator of the various programs in which I was a student. I would be the first ever hired Medical Laboratory Technician, ASCP with the Chicago Public School System which is another NFP venture. I served there for nine years, and later became employed at Morton Career Academy as a school guidance counselor and health career teacher – another NFP. I served a total of twelve (12) years with the CPS system in Chicago. Afterwards, I accepted my calling to ministry, and I became an ordained minister at a church on the west side of Chicago – another NFP stint.

The church housed and operated a community social center agency that had a youth program, food distribution, mentoring program, counseling, and other activities. I held a position as the program director – another NFP stint. I would serve a total of nineteen (19) years at that ministry and moved forward to serve at other churches and social service agencies. Later, I had the opportunity to serve as a chaplain at jails and prisons. Yes, another NFP setting.

So you see, there are different types of NFPs. We are surrounded by them and the NFPs greatly impact our lives daily. Several years later, I started up two NFPs, and later became a NFP consultant and assist people to open NFPs by incorporating and obtaining their 501(c)(3) tax-exempt determination.

What do all these places have in common? They all serve and help people. There is no self-gain or profiting. In each instance, I received a salary, but nothing to make me a millionaire as one would have the opportunity of being if they hang their shingles in the For Profit business. So, there you have it. Unknowingly, I had worked and served in NFP for over thirty (30) years of my life. Now, I am helping others to serve as well. I am known also as a For Profit also known as FP business. I am now on the other side of the corporation arena.

I wrote this book because when I ventured out to start up my first NFP, I could not find detailed information in the setup process. I would find a piece of information here or a piece of information there. I found out a lot of things on the administrative side of NFP by trial and error. After becoming a consultant, many clients trying to obtain funding, embarked on bits and pieces as well. Each ended up with fines or missing major elements in their set ups. There were a lot of doubling back, and cementing cracks in their foundations because each one lacked the knowledge that was needed.

I visited a lot of bookstores and there would be a few books on the shelves and the books were outdated. So, I decided to put together a step-by-step instruction manual in putting a NFP together to help people tie-up loose ends. However, laws and regulations are constantly changing, so it's very important that service providers, especially administrative staff, stay abreast of new policies by periodically checking websites of the Secretary of State, Attorney General's Office, and service to the Internal Revenue. In addition, it's important to have a membership with NFP associations, and to attend seminars sharing the latest that has come out of the Capitol in Washington. One must stay up-to-date about what is new on the Horizon especially when we elect new presidents.

Whenever, we have new presidents, there is also a new administration, new cabinet members, etc., therefore, resulting in new policies and regulations in all industries especially the NFPs. The presiding pages will give you insights and food-for-thought in regards to NFP. You may decide after reading this book that a NFP is not for you. That is okay. It's best to know than to invest hundreds and often thousands of dollars into a NFP venture. Whatever the case, you may now begin your journey.

I have been intrigued by NFP. The NFP career route is for those that want to make a difference in SOMEONE's WORLD, whether a single mom, a lonely senior, a troubled youth, and an ex-offender seeking to re-enter society looking for a second chance. If you are a people person this is the career path for you. If you do not like working with the public, PLEASE, PRETTY PLEASE, keep walking because you will do more harm than good. After reading this book, please ponder, and do a self-evaluation as to whether this would be for you.

What are the pitfalls? Long hours, low wages, sacrifices, sleepless nights, overload of cases, and shoe-string budgets. You must be inventive, creative, resourceful, and an innovator. In addition, you need to be tenacious, resilient, persistent, and a warrior. You cannot be a whiner. You must see the glass half full. You must fight to the death. Some things you will not and have not learned in college.

You may have degrees, experiences, good communication written and oral, including soft skills. All those are great skills to have but are still not enough. You must be willing to run through troops and leap over walls. You must be that energized bunny that we all have seen on commercials. You cannot be a quitter. You must stay focused to succeed if not you will be crushed so do the world and all of us a favor, examine yourself as to whether the NFP arena is for you. Examine your motives and your intent as well.

What are the benefits? You get to see lives change. The NFP can be fulfilling. I saw very sick patients go home healed and happy. As a teacher, I encountered a youth that wanted to kill another student. After our time together discussing the issue, she changed her mind. I helped a foster child get her senior yearbook because her mom did not have any money. I also held a student in my arms whose mom had not been home for days because she walked the street at night. She was able to smile and finish her assignments and graduate. I saw over one thousand clients per month who received food from the food pantry that I operated. Those clients thanked me and the organization for being there for them because they had to decide whether to pay their rent or eat. I saw many men, women, boys, and girls give their lives to Christ. I saw single parents lift their heads in hope for a brighter future not just for their children but for them as well. I shed tears of joy when students walked across the stage and received their high school diplomas and went on to college and received their degrees.

The NFP route can be fulfilling but yet draining at times. In looking back, I would not have had it any other way. While reading this material, make your decision. I applaud you for picking up a copy of this book.

Write some ideas that would benefit the public and how you can help._____

_____

_____

_____

I. THE ORIGIN OF NOT-FOR-PROFIT

Whether one wants to admit it or not, the NFP origin is associated with the Jewish people after the great exodus. Once Jews entered into CANAAN, the promise land, each tribe had their own parcel of land, and each family unit had their own strip of land that had been planted and due a bountiful harvest. The children of Israel were a group of agricultural people. God had commanded them to remember the poor and allow them to glean off the land. And whenever a brother or sister was sold into slavery at an appointed time, they were supposed to be released from their debt and have charity extended toward them. You can read more about the charitable acts that were a requirement to perform in one of the books of Moses entitled Leviticus where laws were given to them by God. We follow many of the Levitical laws today. You can read about sanitary laws, dietary laws, civil laws, moral laws, spiritual laws, etc.

If we fast forward passed biblical times we will discover that charitable, educational, and religious NFPs are thousands of years old, and the largest is the Catholic Church. Within the United States of America, NFP establishments date back as far as colonial times. Amongst the first is Harvard University. In fact, over ninety percent (90%) of the NFPs also known as non-governmental organizations have been established since 1950; however, NFP did not become regulated and unified until the early 1970.

In addition, numerous churches in England conducted charitable activities. Each church formed a group of people who did not want to be ministers or church workers that wanted to do charitable activities outside of the confinement of the walls of the church. In other words, they wanted the opportunity to provide services without having to be a church. The scope is wide from small grass roots with no assets, to NFP with multimillion dollar structures, universities, and religious orders. The NFP supports a range from private contributions, sales from goods and some services, grants, and governmental agencies.

The term NFP also covers sorority, fraternity, masons, associations, cemeteries, civic groups, scientific research groups, hospitals, symphonies, and even alcoholic anonymous. Any group that has a charitable aspect can be deemed a NFP and is eligible to apply for the 501(c)(3) tax-exempt status which is so coveted.

What did you get from The Origin of NFP: _____

_____
_____
_____
_____
_____
_____
_____

II. TYPES OF NOT-FOR-PROFIT

Since NFP has been around for centuries throughout

the world, there are many different types of NFPs and some would surprise you. The most common are churches, ministries, hospitals, social service agencies, and most schools. There are lodges, civil centers, the arts, cultural centers, multimedia centers, research organizations, and others. You may wonder how a hospital is a NFP yet people are billed? Well, when you are serving a community and you do not turn anyone away, services are being rendered to those who can pay and to those who cannot pay. Hospitals are also known to provide free health educational workshops, free health fairs, free screenings usually diabetes, blood pressure, mammogram, and other services to the community. A NFP must include some free services.

Annually, hospitals review records and forgive a percentage of large debts; therefore, they can be listed as a NFP. However, not all NFPs are tax-exempt. You must qualify and read the "IRS Publication 557" for eligibility requirement. What is certain is that you must be incorporated prior to filing Form 1023 which is also known as the 501(c)(3) application. Should you apply, it is not guaranteed. It is imperative to meet the standards for the 501(c)(3) determination. If you plan to still run your NFP, although, you do not meet the standards for the 501(c)(3), it is a requirement to incorporate regardless.

It is imperative to become incorporated with the state in which you intend for the NFP to operate and provide services. If you operate and are caught, you will be shut down, receive a fine and penalty, and be barred in some instances of ever operating a NFP. Now that you are aware of the legalities, you need to decide what services you intend to provide and to what target group, along with the specific location.

Think of a name you want for the organization. Once you select a name for the NFP, a name check must be conducted with the secretary of state. If the name is used by another organization, it is not available to you. However, you do not have to lose heart. If it's a name you really like, you can either add another name, or number to it which would distinguish it from that NFP. You must type or write in black ink the selected name for the NFP that you and the board have chosen.

What form do you have to fill-out to apply for a 501(c)(3) status: _____

_____

Write several business names that would be a good name for your NFP:

_____

_____

_____

_____

_____

_____

III. Name

You may choose any name as long as it is distinguishable from the name of an existing corporation, a foreign corporation authorized to conduct business affairs in the state in which the NFP will provide services. No name shall contain the words Democrat, regular democrat, democratic, republican or the name of any other established political party unless consent is given by the State Central Committee of such established party. The name that is chosen for a NFP must end with the letters NFP if the corporate name contains any word or phrase that indicates or implies that the corporation is organized for any purpose other than a purpose for which corporations may be organized under the Business Corporation Act. You may find out the availability of a name by writing or calling the Secretary of State's office in your state. A preliminary check also may be done on the Secretary of State's website in the state the NFP will be ran.

You may include a brief written request, listing the name and a brief description of the corporate purpose. You may reserve a name, if available for a period of ninety (90) days for a fee. You must submit a written request that list the name and a brief description of the NFP purpose. In other words, explain why the NFP was formed. There are no limitations to the number of times you can reserve a name.

IV. Board

The NFP does not belong to you or the board members. All NFPs belong to the people of that state for which the NFP resides. Every NFP must have a board, and it is suggested that the initial board consists of three members. It is in the first meeting that you discuss the name, vision, mission, program activities, and the target population that you will provide services. You are not limited to having three board members; however, your board members should be in odd numbers.

Although board members can live in other states and even countries; however, one must be a resident in which the NFP resides. Your board members can be professionals such as doctors, lawyers, CPAs, etc., and also can include community members, activists, and others. Your board can be one race or multicultural. It is suggested that you have a mixture of professionals and nonprofessionals, male & female, multicultural, and different socio-economic backgrounds. Whatever the case, you will need a working board.

The board should be a group of people that bring talents, knowledge, skills, abilities, and DEFINITELY MONEY also known as FUNDINGS, and essential contacts into the organization. You do not want dead weight on your board of directors. The governmental entities such as the Secretary of State, IRS, and others only recognize the position of President, Secretary, Treasurer, and Directors of the organization. Any other titles are known as in-house. In addition, you should give each person a description of their anticipated position, and a set of Bylaws which also describe their duties and the laws that govern your organization.

Should the number of your board members be an even or odd number: _____

The laws that govern your NFP are called: _____

_____

_____

V. MINUTES

Prior to incorporating, you should take minutes that show your intent of formation of a NFP. The minutes should go as following:

- Date of meeting;
- Location of meeting place;
- Time of meeting;
- Open meeting with Robert Rules for parliamentary meetings;
- Those present;
- Intent of meeting;
- List of what was covered;
- Notation of being an initial meeting;
- Selection of officers;
- Selection of a registered agent;
- Selection of location of the NFP;
- NFP Vision Statement;
- NFP Mission Statement;
- Program narratives (organization intended target population and activities);
- Resolution to any conflicts that occurred in the meeting;
- Forwarding of topics for next meeting;
- Next tentative meeting date;
- Name and title of person that took notes; and

- End of meeting.

INTENT OF FORMATION OF A NFP
MEETING MINUTES

DATE OF MEETING	____/____/_____
LOCATION OF MEETING PLACE	_____
TIME OF MEETING	_____
OPEN MEETING WITH ROBERT RULES FOR PARLIAMENTARY	_____
THOSE PRESENT	NAME:_____ TITLE _____
	NAME:_____ TITLE _____
	NAME:_____ TITLE _____
	NAME:_____ TITLE _____
	NAME:_____ TITLE _____
	NAME:_____ TITLE _____
	NAME:_____ TITLE _____
	NAME:_____ TITLE _____
	NAME:_____ TITLE _____
	NAME:_____ TITLE _____
	NAME:_____ TITLE _____

Not-For-Profit Business

NAME:_____ TITLE _____

NAME:_____ TITLE _____

NAME:_____ TITLE _____

INTENT OF MEETING
_____
_____
_____
_____

LIST OF WHAT WAS COVERED
1._____
2._____
3._____
4._____
5._____
6._____
7._____
8._____

NOTATION OF BEING AN INITIAL MEETING
_____
_____

SELECTION OF OFFICERS

NAME:_____ TITLE _____

NAME:_____ TITLE _____

NAME:_____ TITLE _____

NAME:_____ TITLE _____

NAME:_____ TITLE _____

NAME:_____ TITLE _____

NAME:_____ TITLE _____

NAME:_____ TITLE _____

Not-For-Profit Business

NAME:_____ TITLE _____

NAME:_____ TITLE _____

NAME:_____ TITLE _____

NAME:_____ TITLE _____

NAME:_____ TITLE _____

SELECTION OF A REGISTERED AGENT _____

SELECTION OF LOCATION OF THE NFP _____
_____
_____

NFP VISION STATEMENT _____
_____
_____
_____
_____
_____
_____
_____

NFP MISSION STATEMENT _____
_____
_____
_____
_____
_____
_____
_____

PROGRAM NARRATIVES (ORGANIZATION INTENDED TARGET POPULATION AND ACTIVITIES)

POPULATION_____
_____
_____
_____
_____

ACTIVITIES_____
_____

NOT-FOR-PROFIT BUSINESS

_____
_____
_____
_____
_____
_____

RESOLUTION TO ANY CONFLICTS THAT OCCURRED IN THE MEETING

_____
_____
_____
_____
_____
_____
_____
_____
_____
_____
_____
_____
_____
_____

FORWARDING OF TOPICS FOR NEXT MEETING

_____
_____
_____
_____
_____
_____
_____

NEXT TENTATIVE MEETING DATE

_____/_____/_____

NAME AND TITLE OF PERSON THAT TOOK NOTES

NAME:_____ TITLE _____

END OF MEETING

_____
_____
_____
_____
_____
_____
_____

It is during this initial board meeting that those who are present and selected to serve as officials and directors, can sign the incorporation papers. Information regarding the incorporation papers will be covered later.

The organization secretary is responsible for typing, and filing away the minutes of the organization, which is now a legal document that can be subpoenaed by the court system. One month before the next board meeting, letters are to be mailed to board members along with previous minutes, and an agenda which list items to be discussed and covered in the upcoming meetings.

List names of officials and directors of the NFP:

_____

_____

_____

_____

_____

_____

_____

VI. Vision Statement

Every NFP should have a vision statement. It is generally futuristic and describes where the organization would like to be in five (5), ten (10), and twenty (20) years. A vision statement provides the future state of an organization. Below is an example of a Vision Statement:

FRESH START NFP Vision Statement:

The FRESH START NFP will have national offices throughout the United States of America which will offer agglomerate of program services to provide recovery treatment programs which will result in a fresh start in life.

Write your NFP Vision Statement:

_____

_____

_____

_____

_____

Write your NFP Vision Statement in 5 years, 10 years, and 20 years:

5 Years: _____

_____

_____

_____

10 Years: _____

_____

_____

_____

_____

20 Years: _____

_____

_____

_____

_____

VII. MISSION STATEMENT

Every nonprofit organization must have a mission statement. It is generally one or two sentences that clearly state the organization's purpose. A mission statement provides the present state of an organization. Below is an example of a mission statement:

> **FRESH START NFP Mission Statement:**
>
> All people have the right to be self-sufficient with self-esteem. Still today, many people suffering from alcohol and drug abuse are lacking a sense of self-worth, because they cannot pay for adequate treatment for recovery.
>
> FRESH START offers these people an opportunity for recovery and positive changes through affordable, effective counseling and therapy to restore an individual's sense of responsibility and self-worth.

Write your Mission Statement Purpose:

_____

_____

_____

_____

_____

VIII. SECRETARY OF STATE

Every state within the United States has a state agency known as the Secretary of State. Whatever state you intend to incorporate the NFP organization, should be done through that particular secretary of state's office. You just simply ask for an application to form a NFP.

If you are not incorporated and decide to operate as a NFP and it is found out by the state, you can be shut down and be given a hefty fine. The NFP must be recognized on the state level first by the Secretary of State.

IX. ARTICLES OF INCORPORATION

The document that is used to incorporate the NFP is known as the Articles of Incorporation, now there are other documents of formations. However, the most common formation is the articles of incorporation and that will be discussed later in the book. Articles of Incorporation is usually a one sheet document front and back and is relatively easy to fill out. We will explore each section. In order to file this document with the Secretary of State, a filing fee is charged.

A. Corporation Name and Address

There are two types of corporations in the United States: foreign and domestic. Foreign corporations are those that operate outside of the United States, although, their paperwork has been completed within the states. There are domestic corporations which are those NFPs that are located and operate within the United States.

Under the term domestic corporations, you have what is known as For-Profit (order my book titled "For-Profit Business" for more information) and NFP also known as Nonprofit. We are covering in this book NFP formation and other pertinent information to assist you in your startup venture. When the focus is on NFP, there were a variety that were covered earlier such as churches, some schools, hospitals, cultural centers, art institutes, museums, lodges, etc.

Before filing the Articles of Incorporation, it is best to do a name check. I would like to share a situation where a name check was not conducted and an organization ended up in court, heavily fined, and ordered to not use the name. An overzealous community member with limited NFP experience did not do a name check. Well, five years down the line that individual had left the position and the organization received a letter from the Secretary of State to inform the organization that the name was already in use. The organization received a fine.

Here is another incident: There was a social service agency with the same identical name as someone who had the name first and had been operating for over twenty-five

(25) years. The executive director of that organization contacted the agency and requested that they change the name. Well, they refused to do so and were dragged into court. The judge ruled in favor of the older NFP and fined the organization. The court also told the other NFP to cease operating in that name. The organization regrouped, kept the name and added some distinguishing factors to it. Remember if a name is being used and you like it, you can keep it by adding to it; which is legal.

List Several Names that Describe Your NFP:

_____

_____

_____

_____

Next list the principal office location of the NFP. It can be an administrative office where there is no programs onsite or programs can be taking place onsite. Some NFPs have several locations; although, you must provide the main location on the application.

Address of the Main Location is:

_____

_____

_____

_____

_____

List Other Locations Here, if any:

_____

_____

_____

_____

_____

B. Registered Agent

The purpose of requiring each corporation to maintain a registered agent and a registered location is for public record where service of process against the corporation and such person may be found. This person also is the one to whom official correspondence may be found. Also, this person is the one to whom official correspondence from the Secretary of State is sent. However, there are qualifications that must be met to be a registered agent.

C. Registered Agent's Address Qualifications

A registered agent must be a residence of the state for which the NFP will reside and provide services. The registered agent must be at least eighteen (18) years of age. The registered agent can also be a listed corporation.

The registered office of the agent must be within the state of which the NFP resides and a street or road address is to be provided, A Post Office box number is not acceptable. After listing the corporate name and address, a registered agent must be listed. This is no more than a contact person. This is a person who receives the organization's mail, and serves as a contact. You can either use the registered agent personal address or the address of the NFP location. If changes need to be made in regards to either, the registered agent or the office, the change must be reported as soon as possible. Prompt reporting of changes is important to ensure that correspondence will not be delayed or lost.

You must select the intended duration of the NFP. The duration is the period of time you plan to be incorporated. The duration is perpetual, unless otherwise stated in the Articles of Incorporation. The term perpetual means ongoing and endless.

D. Initial Board Members

The board members' printed names, signatures, addresses, cities, states, and zip codes must appear on the incorporation papers. Caution: if you are setting up and spearheading your organization, and this is your vision, you must be included on the board. It is suggested that you be the registered agent as well; or you can assign that task to another and appear on the board only. However, if you appear as the registered agent only and not on the board, you have no voice and you will not be able to offer any suggestions and ideas.

E. Project Activities

You must state that your organization is charitable or a private foundation, describe your target population, and the services to be rendered. The target population described can be children and youths, homeless, victims of domestic violence, seniors, women, men, gang members, etc. Describe the services to be rendered such as shelter also known as dormitory, supportive services, case managements, arts, housings, after school programs, transportations, daycare, etc. The sharing of this information should be found in both your vision and mission statements. You are revealing the purpose for which the NFP is formed.

F. SIGNATURES

It is important that you have the signatures, addresses, cities, states, and zip codes of the board members on the incorporation document. The paperwork should be filled out in duplicates. If you do not have their signatures, the application will not be filed. Once you are processed, the state will keep a copy and stamp the other forms and send to you with an announcement letter that you are now incorporated in the state for which the NFP resides.

X. CERTIFICATE OF GOOD STANDING

This is a needful document especially when it is time for you to seek funding. A Certificate of Good Standing is a document that will let the funder know that the NFP for which the state resides is still incorporated and not dissolved. Contact the secretary of state in your area to obtain the certificate of good standing. A small fee is required.

XI. IN CONCLUSION OF NFP INCORPORATION

The information given above describes the information which all states have in their incorporation papers. The formats may be slightly different but each form contains the same requirements that are stated above. In addition, there may be a question asking if you are a type of an association, in which you should answer accordingly. In most cases, the answer will be "No."

Due to everyone being cost-conscious, states are streamlining and have created one form where you can check off NFP or FP then proceed to answer the applicable questions that pertains to the NFP.

Becoming a NFP organization is like a two-sided coin. It will benefit the public and also be rewarding seeing others change for the betterment of mankind. The team effort of the Board Members will help make the NFP organization effective.

From time to time, refer back to the Vision Statement and Mission Statement to be sure you are focused on the reason the NFP was formed.

If you chose not to obtain a 501(c)(3), taxes will be due. In the following section, I will discuss further how to obtain a 501(c)(3).

NFP 501(c)(3)

I. WHY A 501(c)(3)

Why a 501(c)(3)? Is it necessary to apply for the 501(c)(3) from the internal revenue service when you are applying for a NFP? No. Once you are incorporated by the state in which your NFP resides, you can legally operate within your state as a NFP. However, if anyone gives you donations, it is not tax deductible. In other words, there are no write-offs for the individual also known as private contributors, businesses, foundations, or funders. Therefore, it is somewhat of a *catch-22* (a dilemma where there is no escape) situation. It has also been cited that churches are not required to have it either once again, it's a *catch-22*.

II. IRS

The IRS is huge and it is very important that you contact and have your paperwork sent to the correct division, and that you speak with the correct IRS agent. I have heard so many horror stories. We will look at one case before concluding the information that will be shared. The IRS has two (2) main divisions when it comes to tax reporting. The FOR PROFIT and the NOT-FOR-PROFIT. The reporting of both is different. When you have a 501(c)(3), you are tax-exempt. The IRS wants you to file information of donations that comes into your organization so keep a record of the sponsors and the amounts of each donation. Those records of donations are called gross receipts.

Donors' Name:
Donation Amount:
Address:
Email Address:
Phone No.:

Donors' Name:
Donation Amount:
Address:
Email Address:
Phone No.:

Donors' Name:
Donation Amount:
Address:
Email Address:
Phone No.:

Donors' Name:
Donation Amount:
Address:
Email Address:
Phone No.:

Donors' Name:
Donation Amount:
Address:
Email Address:
Phone No.:

Donors' Name:
Donation Amount:
Address:
Email Address:
Phone No.:

Donors' Name: _____
Donation Amount: _____
Address: _____
Email Address: _____
Phone No.: _____

Donors' Name: _____
Donation Amount: _____
Address: _____
Email Address: _____
Phone No.: _____

Churches are exempt from filing what is known as an annual report. All other charities as well as public and private foundations are required to submit an annual report. The filing of the annual report is completed on a 990, 990 EZ, or 990-N Electronic Filing. The 990 is a full form to record monetary and properties donations. The 990 EZ is a short form that is usually one page. You file either of these when donations has been $50,000 or more. There is the 990-N Electronic Filing, which is an electronic form to be completed online and filled out when the organization has received funding under $50,000. If you miss three (3) consecutive years of filing, the 501(c)(3) is revoked.

It will also be helpful to subscribe to the IRS newsletter and periodically check www.IRS.gov to read continual updates. IRS is constantly making changes in their policies and as stated in an earlier section; whenever we elect a new president, policies change as well as a new administration. The lack of knowledge of the most current best practices will not cut it. If you do not keep up-to-date and a violation happens, there may be hefty penalties. When you log on to the government's website, you can search for

CHARITIES and NON-FOR-PROFITS in order to review updates.

As mentioned before, FOR PROFIT. The FOR PROFITs are required to complete tax reporting of the earnings of their business(es), and pay their taxes according to their business structure. In my book titled, "For Profit," I will cover more information regarding tax reporting of earnings.

III. BENEFITS OF 501(C)(3)

Now, I will share a case study about Pastor Yakes and the XYZ Church of God & Christ. A new member who is an accountant, which was excited, approached the pastor of the church asking if the church had been paying any taxes. The pastor allows the member to review all church fiscal records. After reviewing the records, the accountant concludes and prepares a tax report on behalf of the church for the pastor. Several months later, the pastor is contacted by the IRS and is informed that a substantial amount of taxes is owed.

I was in a restaurant when the pastor approached me remembering the type of work that I do and we set up an appointment. He confides in me the dilemma. After reviewing all records that he has a 501(c)(3), I reminded him therefore, the contributions are tax-exempt, and all he has to do is inform the IRS and give the For Profit Tax Division a copy of his 501(c)(3) determination letter and the nightmare would go away. He goes back to the member who is an accountant and the accountant chose to do something else. Three (3) days later, the IRS is on his doorstep to confiscate the church, rental properties, his home, and van.

A most common problem that I have found is that people consult lawyers, CPAs, and accountants that do not have a NFP background. If you are going to use the services of any of these professionals, make sure someone is knowledgeable and experienced in the NFP arena. The accountant submitted documentation to the IRS as if the church was a FOR PROFIT business instead of presenting the church as a NOT-FOR-PROFIT with a 501(c)(3).

Why is the 501(c)(3) important? _____

_____

_____

IV. EMPLOYER IDENTIFICATION NUMBER (EIN)

After becoming incorporated through your state, you need to move forward and obtain an EIN which stands for Employer Identification Number. Just think of it as a business social security number. An EIN is assigned to your NFP so that it will be identifiable and distinguished from other organizations. The EIN is very important for without it your 501(c)(3) application will not be processed. If you ever have to contact the IRS to discuss your organization, the first thing the IRS agent asks before pulling up your file is, the EIN.

This number is also important in tax reporting season. Although you are a 501(c)(3) tax-exempt organization, you are still required to submit a report to the IRS. This informs the IRS of the amount of gross receipts that your organization attained. Thus, you are reporting the amount of donations that came into the organization.

If your organization is a 501(c)(3) and it receives below $50,000, you would file taxes electronically using the 990E-Postcard. If your organization received over $50,000, you must submit either the 990 or 990 EZ by mail. This is subject to change because most companies are doing everything online.

Please note, if the tax year ends in December, the deadline for completing and submitting any of the 990s **is May 15th**. If the tax year ends in July, the deadline for completing and submitting any of the 990s is **by December 15th**. Five months after your fiscal year ends and on the 15th day.

If you do not attain the 501(c)(3) tax-exempt status any donations over $650 that comes into the organization, taxes are required to be paid both to the state and to the federal government.

The benefit of the 501(c)(3) determination tax-exempt services is that an organization is exempt from paying both state and federal taxes of funding. Hence, when an organization does not have the 501(c)(3) exemption status, whatever funding comes into the organization, state and federal taxes must get paid on those funds.

Another benefit of having the 501(c)(3) status is that your organization will be eligible for sales tax exemption; which means that when you purchase items from a vendor, stores, etc., you will not be required to pay taxes just pay for the purchases.

The purchases must be on behalf of the organization and for organizational purposes only. For example, if you have a youth after school program, the items purchased should reflect the services that are being offered to the youth. Items cannot be purchased for the use of staff, volunteers, or board members but for the target population for which services are intended. The items that can be bought for the organization can range from office equipment, office supplies, household products, personal hygiene products, vehicles, real estates, etc.

The 501(c)(3) is also helpful in assisting organizations that own real estates to be exempt from paying property taxes, and water bills. You must check within your state and see all that is offered to 501(c)(3) NFP. The 501(c)(3) can be used to obtain free or reduce leasing opportunities such as office space and rental for gala events.

The 501(c)(3) organizations are also eligible to use meeting rooms of public libraries for free. The park district, offers reduce rates for rentals of events. The United States Postal Service offers reduce bulk mail rate to 501(c)(3) NFP.

1. What comes first the 501(c)(3) or the EIN?

_____

2. When are you able to file your gross receipts (taxes) online? _____

_____

_____

_____

3. What is one of the benefits of having a tax-exempt status?

_____

_____

V. 501(C)(3) APPLICATION

The 501(c)(3) application is also known as Form 1023. It looks like a booklet and comes with an instruction section. The instruction section is the beginning pages, and there is the actual application that has nine sections that consist of twelve (12) pages. It usually takes over forty (40) hours to complete the pages.

Page one (1) consist of the organization's general information, Page two (2) is where you would answer questions as to whether you are a corporation and if so which type, if you have bylaws, including questions about clauses, there is a section to list the board members, their positions, addresses, and if the board members are to receive compensations. Page three (3) has questions about the highest paid employee or contractor to receive salary. Next is a series of conflict of interest, policies, and other questions are asked from page four (4) to page eight (8). On page eight (8) there are questions about the organization's assets if you have any and whether you are a public charity or a private foundation. On page nine (9) you will find a projected budget which will reflect your activities, how will your organization receive and support your programs, and the remaining pages require an authorized officer's position and signature.

In addition, there is a checklist to ensure that you have everything in the envelope which you plan to mail off to the IRS. The checklist range from organization information, EIN #, power of attorney, schedules, etc. Just go to IRS.gov and do a search for Form 1023 and take a look at the entire application. Once the application is completed, everything is placed inside a large envelope addressed to the IRS.

Now, the IRS charges what is called a user fee which is really a processing fee for them to review and release the 501(c)(3). Over one billion people apply for this document yearly; however, approximately 750,000 people actually are approved for the 501(c)(3) status. It is a tedious process and one must be familiar with the NFP language. NFPs are usually turned down for the following reasons:

1) Do not follow directions,
2) Do not answer all the questions,
3) Activities are not exempt activities,
4) Lack of NFP language,
5) Do not have a purpose clause,
6) Do not have a dissolution clause,
7) Do not enclose or forward bylaws,
8) Conflict of interest within the application,
9) Did not enclose the user fee, or
10) Did not enclose the appropriate user fee.

Unfortunately, some people do not know how to follow instructions which results in being denied. You are expected to answer ALL questions no matter if you feel that it was answered in another section of the application.

Another reason for denial is that activities sound more like a for profit activity; therefore, making an organization sound like a business. In addition, it is wise to have someone with an educational background and experience or both, to complete the application.

Language! Language! Language! If you are not familiar with the NFP arena, you will not be able to accurately and satisfactorily answer the questions; same thing with proposal writing. The application and your Bylaws require a Purpose Clause. What is a purpose clause? It is the reason for which your organization was formed. The Purpose Clause is the activities that you describe with your Secretary of State.

A Dissolution Clause is also required within the 501(c)(3) application and the bylaws. You must have a dissolution clause that states that no one associated with the NFP whether an officer, board member, director, staff, or volunteers will not profit from the NFP. In the event that the NFP has to be dissolved, all monetary assets, in kind, equipment, supplies, properties, etc. must be given as donations to a NFP that has the similar mission of the defunct NFP. In other words, no one can decide to take computers, furniture, supplies, or items home after the NFP folds. There is no ownership in a NFP. The NFP belongs to the people within that state. Bylaws governs and set laws for the organization. It is also important to periodically update the organization's Bylaws.

In America on September 11 (911), congress passed a ruling that it must be included in all Bylaws that the NFP, for which you have been entrusted to oversee, will not do business nor allow networking or alliances with known terrorists. A statement of such must appear in the Bylaws along with a link that is provided. The link has a listing of a database of thousands of identified terrorists.

Recently, our government passed laws legalizing same sex marriage. If you are a church or ministry, you are required to put in your Bylaws that you will not conduct marriage ceremonies to people of the same sex along with biblical scriptures. Otherwise, you will have to do so, and it will be unlawful for you not to. I recommend that you periodically update your Bylaws especially when there is changing of the guards, hence a new administration.

Go to the IRS.gov website and monitor the public charities section. Register for the e-newsletter so you can stay up-to-date on information. I cannot stress enough the importance of staying informed.

In 2010 a lot of NFPs were caught off guard when a ruling was enacted that if a NFP missed three consecutive years of filing their 990s annual report, the 501(c)(3) will be revoked. In order to get reinstated, a new application will have to be submitted stating the reason why it was revoked and a plan explaining preventive measures to avoid being revoked again. In addition, a form for reinstatement must be completed, along with a fee of $400, $850, or whatever user fee is being charged based on your organization's budget. Please keep in mind, the user fee is subject to change, and I want to encourage you to retain the 501(c)(3) status.

There is a filing fee for the 501(c)(3) application. In 2004 the user fee was $150 for an organization's budget under $10,000, and $500 for an organization's budget of over $10,000. In the year 2016, if an organization's budget is under $10,000, the user fee was $400. If the budget is over $10,000, the user fee was $850. So I hope that you see urgency in getting your NFP organization filed under a 501(c)(3).

Another reason that applicants are denied the tax-exempt status, the application shows conflict of interests. The IRS frowns on a board that consists of all family members. Family members can serve on the board but cannot make up the total board. The 501(c)(3) application will be declined

Another conflict of interest would be if the organization purchase and/or lease, goods, services, etc. from an officer, board member, director, staff, or volunteer. This is also a conflict of interest. In addition, there is a series of questions that can identify a conflict of interest. Believe it or not, terrorist activities are also a conflict of interest which can result in an investigation being launched against your NFP organization.

Another reason applications are denied the 501(c)(3) status, people forgot to include the user fee or the appropriate user fee, and/or the budget and program activities are not equivalent. The activities within the program services prices would be higher but being reported lower in describing the financials, therefore, resulting in a decline of the application.

Most of the time, an agent will send a letter about an issue that needs to be resolved about the application and usually gives thirty (30) days to resolve. If you need additional time, you can request an extension. The agent will also give you a particular window, usually a month, and if you successfully answered and addressed the issues at hand, the state will release the 501(c)(3) application within two (2) to four (4) weeks after the review.

Once an application is completed, there is a certain order in which the IRS requires each item to be placed inside the envelope. The following list is the requirement:

1) A letter size envelope which encloses the user fee in a cashier's check or money order (check irs.gov for the exact amount),
2) Check off list,
3) 501(c)(3) application also known as Form 1023,
4) Articles of Incorporation and amendments if applicable,
5) Bylaws,
6) Conflict of Interest Policy,
7) Program Narrative,
8) Fundraising Activity,
9) Any schedule if applicable (*e.g.,* churches and schools),
10) Additional information for churches, and
11) The signature of one board member preferably the president is required.

Not following the above order will result in a delay of your application in being reviewed and approved for the 501(c)(3) tax-exempt status.

The IRS does not want anything stapled, cut, or bound. In regards to the user fee, the IRS wants the fee to be placed in an envelope in front of the application. The check off list is for your benefit. If there are any amendments to the articles of incorporation, please include them. In addition, the IRS requires that when you are incorporating your NFP, a document is included which describes both the purpose and dissolution clauses that describes a dissolution clause and a statement that no one would profit from the NFP. The state is not going to tell you that. It is an IRS requirement. You must be aware and submit it along with the incorporation papers that you file. You must include a policy as to how conflict of interest is going to be avoided in the NFP and all associated with the NFP need to be aware of the policy and it should be enforced.

The program narrative consists of the activities or services in which you intend to provide, how often, what do that activity or service entails, who are the activities and services intended, and how many hours will be worked toward rendering of the services or activities. You may want to do a chart or diagram to make it easier for the IRS agent to visualize.

If you are a school, daycare, church, or housing service provider, additional information will be required and you must determine which schedule within the 501(c)(3) application applies to you. Fill out the various questions that are pertinent to the mission, activities, and services of the NFP.

Unfortunately, people forget to sign the application for the 501(c)(3) tax-exempt determination. Therefore, the process cannot be completed although the application has a status of being satisfactorily reviewed. Usually when items are missing from the application it can result in a six (6) to eight (8) months delay before you are contacted by mail.

List items that your NFP already owns:

_____

_____

_____

_____

_____

_____

_____

_____

List items that you need to acquire in order to complete the previous list.

_____

_____

_____

_____

_____

_____

VI. Bylaws

The Internal Revenue Service requires three items to be in your Bylaws that are mandatory. Listed below are the items:

1) You must have a purpose clause. A purpose clause is simply giving the reason for which the organization was formed,
2) The target population to be served, the activities, programs, or program services to be rendered, and
3) The Dissolution clause.

If you do not have these items you will be automatically declined for the 501(c)(3) determination tax-exempt status.

The first mandatory item is stating why your organization was formed. You are describing the type of organization that you are such as a church, social service, agency, school, cultural center, or other. You can describe what group of people the organization plans to serve which is known as the target population. The term is self-explanatory, in that you are describing the target population based on their socio-economic status, ethnicity, gender, or other factors which made you select that particular group of people to serve.

Do you want to serve seniors, children, youth, women, men, or those with low to moderate income? Do you want to serve the underprivileged, underserved, or the illiterate? You must list the services or programs that will be available for the target population. Are you going to provide educational services, housing, counseling, case management, reading program, GED, homework hotline, tutoring, or drama classes? Are you going to provide music composition, an afterschool program, shelter, transitional housing, or mentoring? You will need to describe those services which should be listed in your Articles of Incorporation on the state level, and now this will have to be described in the Bylaws of the organization, and the program narrative attachment of Form 1023, also known as, the 501(c)(3) application.

The second mandatory item is the purpose of the NFP. The purpose will state the activities. What are you going to do with the NFP? The activities can be a school program, mentoring, after school program, educational services, tutoring, community outreach, senior programs, housing services, food distribution, clothing closet, community garden, and the list goes on and on.

The third mandatory item is the Dissolution Clause. This Clause states that no one (which includes officers, board members, directors, staff, or volunteers) will profit, self-gain, or benefit from the NFP. If the NFP becomes dissolved, the assets of the organization will be transferred to a similar organization as stated earlier in the 501(c)(3) Application Section. What is a similar organization?

A similar organization is one that has the same mission as the organization that has become dissolved. The dissolved organization assets such as monetary, in-kind, properties, equipment, supplies, and any other items that belonged to the organization has to be transferred to a similar organization. So, what does that means? There cannot be a board meeting where you all state, we are out of business and people get up from the table and start taking computers, equipment, supplies, and other items. Also, no one can purchase items in the name of the organization and take it home for other personal and/or business use. You can't buy a vehicle in the name of the organization and it's parked outside your door nightly, or going on a fishing trip with the vehicle. One must avoid personal gain as well as conflict of interest.

Included in the third item of the Bylaws, there must be a statement included that the NFP does not and will not support terrorist activities. There is a link that must appear in your Bylaws that leads to the database with thousands of known terrorists' names, along with their businesses that have been identified by homeland security. If you do not have these three mandatory items within the Bylaws, your application will be declined.

There are other items within the Bylaws such as protocol, officers, and their duties. The Bylaws usually covers how often the board meets. The IRS requires that all boards meet at least annually, I recommend that the board meet on a quarterly basis.

The Bylaws covers how to handle funds, resolve disputes, policies, regulations that discuss how the NFP should operate. The Bylaws should also describe how officers are selected, voted, and/or appointed and how long is the term of officers, etc. You must determine if the organization will have a membership.

A perfect example of a NFP with memberships, are churches. When it comes to operating a NFP with a membership, you must describe how members are selected and what are the requirements? (*E.g.*, members have to do a registration and/or pay dues.) If you want to obtain information in the writing of Bylaws, google "sample of Bylaws for NFP" and a series of information will be available for you to examine and select what will work for the NFP which you have formed. Finally, it is important to update the Bylaws. It is recommended that the Bylaws are updated every three years.

Bylaws govern the organization. There has been situations where NFP's board members were at odds with each other and had to appear in court. The judge will always want to examine the Bylaws and if the situation is not addressed in the bylaws, the judge will make a ruling and it may not be favorable of the offended party. There has been cases where the board was wiped out and new people were appointed by the judge and the founder of the NFP was removed. Not a pretty sight. Therefore, it is important that every possible human issue that would surface should be addressed in the Bylaws. Otherwise, the court system will intercept.

VII. FUNDRAISING

The IRS will require a NFP to have a fundraising plan because they want to know how you intend to secure funds to operate and provide services. Below are several methods of fundraising. You may use some or all of the ideas below, including other creative ideas:

Mail Solicitation- Once you have approval from the Secretary of State and the IRS, you can mail out letters to solicit donations through the United States Postal Office.

Email- You may send out solicitations to your email contacts providing that you avoid spam. Check with your service provider about sending out massive emails for the purpose of solicitation.

Personal Solicitation- You can seek the support of family members, neighbors, and other private contributors to your organization.

Foundation Grants- Once you have the tax-exemption status, you may seek a foundation grant maker who has the same mission statement as your organization. There are millions of foundations that seek to fund NFPs.

Phone Solicitation- You may solicit people by phone for contributions, but you must make sure that they are not on the national Do Not Call list. This may result in your organization being sued.

Organization Website- Your organization will be free to solicit donations through your website. You can put PayPal or other pay buttons and instructions for giving directly on your website.

Other Organization Websites- It is permissible to receive donations from other websites. Hence, your web address can be placed on another company's website where you can receive contributions.

Governmental Grants- You can apply and submit grants to fund your organization's activities. You must register to be eligible to apply. You must obtain a Dun & Bradstreet number and SAM, and research the governmental department that fits your mission. (*E.g.*, the Department of Health & Human Services, Department of Agriculture, and the Department of Public Health.)

The president of the United States has a cabinet. The cabinet consists of twelve (12) people that are the head of twelve (12) governmental agencies and each agency provides grant money. Where does grant money come from? Grant money comes from taxes and from businesses that are looking for tax shelters. They promise to invest in the community in which their business resides and in doing so, tax breaks are given when they issue grants through foundations that are created by them. In addition, banks also issue grants to fund programs implemented by NFPs.

Other areas a NFP can receive funding are social media, Kickstarter, GoFundMe, Indiegogo, and other crowd funding investment angels that are social entrepreneurs. A lot of NFPs host galas, dinners, auctions, bake sales, Ad books, cake walks, candy sales and others. You can also use a kettle like the Salvation Army or have a coin machine at stores and cleaners to raise funds for your activities.

Create two or three fundraising ideas that would help your NFP business:

_____

_____

_____

_____

_____

_____

_____

VIII. Program Narratives

You are expected to provide a program narrative of past, present, or future services to be provided to the NFP's target population. You can do it in either a written narrative or graph format. Whatever the case, you need to list the activities, the staff/volunteers to carry out those activities, description of the activities, how often the activity will be conducted (weekly, bi-weekly, etc.), how much time will go into the activities (*e.g.*, eight (8) hours, thirty (30) minutes, etc.), and what percentage will that activity be in a forty (40) hour work week? Will it be ten percent (10%) of the work week or twenty-five percent (25%)? Next, state whether it is a tax-exempt activity and how will the service cost be handled (fee, grant money, public contributions, etc.). Lastly, who will oversee the program (*e.g.*, Executive Director, Program Director, or Supervisor)?

Program Narrative of the Past is: _____

_____

_____

_____

_____

Program Narrative of the Present is: _____

_____

_____

Program Narrative of the future is: _____

_____

_____

_____

IX. ANNUAL BUDGET

***Form 1023, also known as, the 501(c)(3) application requires start up organizations to present a three (3) year projected budget. This consists of fiscal year beginning and fiscal year ending. There are columns in which items are listed. You would either respond with a numerical figure or zero. In this section of the 501(c)(3) application you can record potential contributions, fundraising costs, salaries, program services, etc., which you must give a dollar amount.

What constitutes a budget? Rent, leasing, telephones, utilities, insurance, salaries, equipment supplies, office furniture, program services, and more constitute a budget.

On the following page, you will find the first page of Form 1023 which requires your financial data of the NFP.

Form 1023 (Rev. 12-2013) (00) Name: EIN: -   Page **9**

Part IX Financial Data

For purposes of this schedule, years in existence refer to completed tax years. If in existence 4 or more years, complete the schedule for the most recent 4 tax years. If in existence more than 1 year but less than 4 years, complete the statements for each year in existence and provide projections of your likely revenues and expenses based on a reasonable and good faith estimate of your future finances for a total of 3 years of financial information. If in existence less than 1 year, provide projections of your likely revenues and expenses for the current year and the 2 following years, based on a reasonable and good faith estimate of your future finances for a total of 3 years of financial information. (See instructions.)

A. Statement of Revenues and Expenses

	Type of revenue or expense	Current tax year	3 prior tax years or 2 succeeding tax years			(e) Provide Total for (a) through (d)
		(a) From .... To	(b) From .... To	(c) From .... To	(d) From .... To	
Revenues	1 Gifts, grants, and contributions received (do not include unusual grants)					
	2 Membership fees received					
	3 Gross investment income					
	4 Net unrelated business income					
	5 Taxes levied for your benefit					
	6 Value of services or facilities furnished by a governmental unit without charge (not including the value of services generally furnished to the public without charge)					
	7 Any revenue not otherwise listed above or in lines 9–12 below (attach an itemized list)					
	8 Total of lines 1 through 7					
	9 Gross receipts from admissions, merchandise sold or services performed, or furnishing of facilities in any activity that is related to your exempt purposes (attach itemized list)					
	10 Total of lines 8 and 9					
	11 Net gain or loss on sale of capital assets (attach schedule and see instructions)					
	12 **Unusual grants**					
	13 Total Revenue Add lines 10 through 12					
Expenses	14 Fundraising expenses					
	15 Contributions, gifts, grants, and similar amounts paid out (attach an itemized list)					
	16 Disbursements to or for the benefit of members (attach an itemized list)					
	17 Compensation of officers, directors, and trustees					
	18 Other salaries and wages					
	19 Interest expense					
	20 Occupancy (rent, utilities, etc.)					
	21 Depreciation and depletion					
	22 Professional fees					
	23 Any expense not otherwise classified, such as program services (attach itemized list)					
	24 Total Expenses Add lines 14 through 23					

Form **1023** (Rev. 12-2013)

X. Conflict of Interest

This subject was mentioned earlier. The IRS frowns upon an all family board of officers, board members, staff, volunteers who provide business services to the NFP in which they serve. It is important to avoid self-gain.

You cannot lease properties to family members. Also, a conflict of interest would be if other organizations are coming in to do fundraisers, operate and sell goods to your organization. Hence, board members cannot profit through the NFP; although, they may have a FP business.

XI. Non-Profit Tax Reporting

Here is where confusion comes into play. A NFP is considered a corporation business; however, a 501(c)(3) organization is exempt from paying state and federal taxes. The staff of the NFP is still responsible to report during the tax season to the IRS. The reporting is totally different from domestic and foreign corporations. The NFPs are required to either complete a 990, 990EZ, or 990E-Post Card similar to completing 1040s. However, what is being reported are the funds that came into the NFP for that fiscal calendar year. For example, if an organization receives over $50,000 in donations, a 990 long hard copy form needs to be completed and submitted. There is the short form 990EZ to use if the focus is only monetary contributions. The long forms are used when you are reporting monetary contributions, properties, arts, etc. If the contribution is less than $50,000 for the 501(c)(3) NFP, the 990E-Post Card needs to be completed online.

These reports must be filed five (5) months after their fiscal year by the 15th day of that month. If your NFP fiscal year ends in December, you need to file the appropriate 990 by May 15th. So far, there are no late fees. Please note: **Since 2010, a ruling was passed that if you missed three (3) consecutive years of filings, the 501(c)(3) will be revoked**. Once again it is very important that you periodically check IRS.gov website for new rulings under public charities that will affect NFPs.

When the NFP is a 501(c)(3) organization who is required to file taxes? _____

_____

_____

What do NFPs have to report? _____

_____

_____

What can cause your 501(c)(3) to be revoked? _____

_____

_____

XII. CHURCHES/OTHERS

Churches are required to submit additional information along with the above information.

Churches are required to submit a tenet of faith, church constitution in addition to church Bylaws, a copy of the lease or proof of ownership of the building, pictures of the sanctuary, printed programs of service, organizational chart, church history, church programs, requirement for Ordination, ministerial leadership training programs, an established weekly Sunday school, membership requirements, and sacrament functions.

Every church is expected to submit a Tenet of Faith which is according to their belief. For example, if the church is Christian based, Protestant, Methodist, etc., the language must appear in the Tenet of Faith. Accordingly, if it is a Christian Church, you believe in the trinity, water baptism, communion, and the Old and New Testament.

The church constitution is similar to the United States Constitution. In your church constitution you are explaining the makeup, structure, principles, arrangement and formation. It also gives the concepts and character of what the church is all about. If the church owns its building, a copy of the deed will have to be submitted to the IRS. If the church is leasing space, a copy of the lease agreement must be submitted to the IRS. The IRS also requires that you take outside and inside pictures of the church building where worship is conducted.

The IRS would also like for you to include in your

application a printed program of your services. Most churches submit their Sunday bulletin that reflects the order of service, and the announcements of bible studies, and other functions and events of the churches.

In addition, the IRS would like an organizational chart which lists the chain of command within the church. In order to be considered for the tax-exempt status for the 501(c)(3), the church must have a board, a pastor, and others listed within the organizational chart. You can also use this chart as a diagram to list the various auxiliaries within the church and the leadership department head who oversees each auxiliary within the church, such as: Deacon and Deaconess Boards, Trustee Board, Praise Team, Missionary Board, Food Ministry, Music Ministry, Usher Board, etc.

The IRS also wants information regarding your church's history. Most churches submit their programs when they host a church anniversary, or they have the history written as a separate document. It is required to list every program that is provided (*e.g.*, Sunday School, Morning Worship, Evening Services, Bible Study, Women's Day, Men's Day, Pastor's Anniversary, Choir Anniversary, events, etc.). Include information regarding the spiritual leader and his/her credentials are required for submission as well. The church is required to have a training program for future ministers. The future ministers are required to complete an application, pay an application fee, take a course of study, and complete the exam.

You also have to report the candidate's first sermon, meetings with the board, and ordinations along with documentation. Each candidate should have a folder and you should have a copy of the curriculum as well. In addition, your church must have a Sunday school for the young and perform sacrament services to qualify for the 501(c)(3) tax-exempt service.

You can have all of the above and exclude Sunday school for the young and the sacrament services and you will be declined. You would be surprised that there are some churches that do not have Sunday school. That is a NO, NO.

What is a sacrament service? Do you conduct weddings? Do you conduct funerals? Do you conduct burials? Do you provide communion? You must provide the above services for the 501(c)(3) determination. In addition, the IRS will want to know your membership count and a number of those that actually show up for services. They will also want to know if the members are permitted to be a part of another ministry. It is required to explain how people can become members of your church.

Are the members required to fill out an application? Are they required to attend a new member's class? Do they have to confess Christ? Are they required to sign a creed to accept membership rules? If so, you must have a measure of discipline. What happens when a member does not conduct themselves as expected? Are they removed from the membership? If so, what is that process to remove them from the membership?

In addition, there is what is known as schedules within the application that churches must provide. You have to complete those schedules by answering questions.

Example of the questions can range from how many members do the church have? Are members permitted to be members of other churches? Does the church have a minister? And other related questions. Once all of the above is addressed, you are ready to submit the 501(c)(3) application.

There are schools, civic centers, lodges, and others that seek the 501(c)(3) determination. What is required is that you complete all twelve (12) pages of the application and the corresponding appropriate schedules for your organization. Schedules are additional forms to list added information that has been requested. Every NFP does not have to submit schedules. Most common ones that do have to submit schedules are churches, daycare centers, housing, and others along with their applications.

Q: Who does your NFP belong to?

A:

Q: Once you file your NFP with the state and on the federal level, is it important to file with the Attorney General's Office?

A:

Q: What is an EIN?

A:

NFP OTHER

I. CHARITABLE POLICY

You are required to have a charitable policy. A charitable policy is a statement that you do not discriminate against a person due to race, age, ethnicity, etc. In addition, list the target population for whom you have and will serve. This charitable policy comes in handy when it's time to request the sales tax-exemption.

II. ATTORNEY GENERAL OFFICE

Every state has an attorney general's office. Most NFPs, once incorporated and receive the 501(c)(3) determination from the IRS, rarely register with the attorney general's office. Why?

Because the board is unaware or do not deem it necessary and feel that as long as the NFP is recognized on both the state and federal level as a NFP, that should be sufficient. However, that is not enough. It is a mandate to be registered with the attorney general's office. You must request a registration form in the State where your NFP resides. You can complete a CO1 and a CO2. If you are a church, you are to complete a CO3.

CO is an abbreviation for charitable organization. Once you are registered, you are placed in the Attorney General's database. Funders check this database to see if you are registered as well as Jesse White's office or the office in the state which you are registered and the IRS database. Failure to register with the Attorney General's office can result in a penalty especially if you collected funds prior to registration. People have paid stiff penalties up to $10,000 or more for receiving donations and not being registered. You must register with the Attorney General's office of your state in which the NFP resides.

III. THE DEPARTMENT OF REVENUE

The Department of Revenue is the department to contact when seeking the sales tax-exemption. There is no fee for the sales tax-exemption. However, make sure that you have reached the sales tax division for NFP.

There is a division that handles domestic corporations and you want to be exempt from taxes, so you have to make sure that you have the right department. (First, you must know that the 501(c)(3) determination letter exempts the donations that are given to the NFP from state and federal taxes.) The 501(c)(3) determination letter does not exempt the NFP from sales taxes. However, the sales tax-exemption letter allows you to not pay taxes on merchandise. The document that exempts NFP from sales taxes comes from the Department of Revenue and every state has that department.

In Illinois the number issued starts with a letter. Once that document is attained, any purchases on behalf of the organization can be exempt from sales taxes. The document can be used to purchase household items, personal hygienic items, cars, properties, etc. sales tax free. If you do conferences, rent facilities, or make purchases, you can obtain sales tax free as well.

What is required? You can apply online or in writing.

When applying on-line, just give the required information. If you apply in writing you must submit a letter; brochure that includes days and hours of operation, services provided, charitable policy, and eligibility requirements for services; a copy of the article of incorporation, and the 501(c)(3). If you are a church, pictures and a copy of your lease or copy of your deed must be included.

How many ways can you apply for sales tax-exemption? And what are they? _____

_____

_____

_____

If you are a church, what are some of the items you need to submit when applying for sales tax-exemption? _____

_____

_____

_____

IV. BUSINESS REGISTRATION

You are required to register your business with your state's Department of Revenue. You can do it online by downloading the form, complete it, and mail in the form to your state Department of Revenue.

V. BUSINESS LICENSE

Usually NFPs are not required to have business

licenses unless products are being sold. Selling merchandise requires a license. For example, some NFPs have vending machines or a coffee café. If that is the case, you are required to have a license because the income that was generated is not tax-free.

Are NFPs required to have a business license?

Yes ____ or No ____

VI. DUN & BRADSTREET

There is a nine-digit identification number to identify your business whether it is a NFP or an FP. This is used to set up a credit profile that lenders and potential partners can review to assess the financial stability of your organization. If you intend to apply for governmental grants, it is mandatory to have this number. If you are a NFP that is applying for governmental grants, it is mandatory that you have what is referred to as a DUNs number. The DUNs number is free.

Is it required to have a DUNs number when operating a NFP? Yes _____ or No _____

Why is it important to have a DUNs number? _____

_____

_____

_____

VII. SAM

If you intend to be a federal contractor, in addition to

the DUNs number, you will need a SAM number; which stands for system award management number. You must apply if planning to submit federal grants. The SAM number is free.

What are some businesses that you can add to the NFP?
_____
_____
_____
_____
_____
_____
_____

Do you have to file taxes on the money you make in the business(es)? Yes _____ or No _____

VIII. UNRELATED BUSINESS ACTIVITIES

There are many NFPs that have businesses that generate income and use revenues to support their mission and to continue to provide services. A good example is the Salvation Army. We know their mission is human services, and the organization provides housing, clothing, and shelter. However, they are well known for their thrift stores which is a business that generates revenue to support their services. Catholic Charities provides social services yet they have day care centers, which is a business. Churches and ministries provide bookstores, restaurants, cafés, day care centers, schools, messenger services, etc. that generates business.

In the above cases, business licenses are required, and the income must be reported on the 990 as unrelated business. What does unrelated business mean? It means that the NFP has this activity to raise funding for their mission but this activity has nothing to do with the NFP mission. There is a section on the 990 to do the reporting of unrelated business.

Of course, taxes must be paid on the state and federal level because those profits are not exempt nor covered by the 501(c)(3).

IX. SUSTAINABILITY

NFPs must be ready to develop a sustainability plan, especially when it's time to seek funding for program activities. Long gone are the endless years of funding.

Foundations do not want to be deemed an ATM machine nor NFP welfare system. In other words, the 501(c)(3) covers charitable activities. Charitable means FREE services that are supported by grants, private donations, sponsorship, contributions, and fundraising distributed to the target population.

For example, if you have a youth program and the children are receiving tutoring, mentoring, seminars and workshops, but you host a skating party and charge a fee, the skating party has nothing to do with tutoring, mentoring, seminars, or workshops. The skating party is not related to the reason that the NFP was formed. Anywhere that you are charging a price for an event, it is an unrelated activity to the NFP's mission.

Funders want to provide funding on a short term scenario, therefore, they are expecting NFPs to have a plan that if they decide not to fund the NFP that the services will not discontinue. In the NFP arena, funders are requesting sustainability programs. Funding can be for one (1) year, two (2) years, three (3) years, and even five (5) years. Some grants are a one-time deal. Other grants you may have to renew through the grant application process annually. The length of how long a NFP can receive funding from a grant maker is determined by the funder. Whatever the case, a plan to sustain services need to be developed.

Some NFPs invest funds that they receive into the stock market. It is legal to do so. How do you think the Catholic Church obtained such huge massive wealth although it's now drying up due to the various lawsuits that they have acquired?

I do not remember which pope, but there was a pope that had a secret meeting with JP Morgan and he handed over several chests filled with contributions not knowing what to do with it. Well, JP Morgan took the funds back in the 1700s and this financial wizard made that denomination rich.

Some NFPs open up businesses that generate income to fund program services. A perfect example, the arts and multicultural centers charge for performances and give lessons. Some NFPs form community gardens and sell vegetables to generate funds. Some NFPs secure properties and rent space in homes and offices to generate funding. There are others that open stores, day care centers, bookstores, cafés, coffee shops, and the list goes on and on.

One must do an assessment and determine how to generate funding inside and outside of the NFP. We are living in times where funders are asking for the secure sustainability plans to be submitted along with proposals.

What are some of the ways you plan to sustain the NFP?

_____

_____

_____

_____

Why is it important? _____

_____

_____

_____

X. COLLABORATIVE ACTIVITIES

The days of the "long rangers" are over. The "long rangers" are those who come to rescue you when your plan does not work. Funders are looking for NFPs to pull their resources together and many grants require multiple NFPs to appear inside the grants. However, NFPs must protect themselves with a Memorandum of Understanding because in the past, NFPs received funding that did not pay out to the others on the grant.

In Closing, now you have explored the possibility of setting up a NFP. Hopefully, the information will jolt and jumpstart you. But guess what? You must now learn how to operate and manage your NFP after the startup phase.

What is a Memorandum of Understanding? _____

_____

_____

You thought that was it? NO. You are only just beginning. Here are some other items to consider.

XI. LIABILITY INSURANCE

Every NFP need liability insurances for several reasons. If someone falls or you are involved in an accident, you will have coverage. The board members and staff need to be covered under liability insurance in case erroneous advice is given to clients or some type of harm is caused by the people that represent the organization. Lastly, most funders want to know if the NFP is covered with liability so that the grant monies will not be a resource to deal with liabilities or lawsuits. If your NFP has a DBA clause (Doing Business As) which creates an FP, coverage will be needed to qualify for bid opportunities with businesses and governmental entities.

Why does a NFP need liability insurance? _____

_____

_____

XII. Brochures/Stationery/Business Cards

Some people jump the gun when it comes to this topic. You should not have business cards, postcards, brochures printed until you are incorporated. I have met people that were not incorporated who had brochures, business cards, and postcards printed while they were working toward becoming legitimate. Others felt that it was too much work and fees to legalize themselves and chose to continue with the business as usual. Once again, if you are operating a NFP and are not incorporated by your secretary of state, and not registered with your state's attorney general office, you can be shut down and receive huge fines. Once you are incorporated, you can proceed to develop, and print your brochures, business cards, and the like whether or not you have the 501(c)(3) determination. Remember, the 501(c)(3) is for tax-exempt purposes.

When is it a great time to print business materials?

_____

_____

_____

XIII. Website/Social Media

Once you are incorporated, you can move forward to hiring a web designer or develop your own web design through self-help. You can google and sites will come up with do it yourself templates. In addition, you can also find companies that will assist you in designing your website for a nominal fee. Vistaprint is a well-known established company that specializes in helping startups. Wix.com offers free websites if you are willing to advertise their name. However, the company appears to be more legitimate when the web address does not include wix.com in the address. Therefore, pay the annual fee. Many NFPs as well as FPs have set up Facebook pages to offer their programs, services, and products.

XIV. PAYROLL

Once you have everything set up, you need employees. There will come a time where you will need full time staff or part time. Once you start issuing pay checks, although, the NFP is exempt from paying state and federal taxes, the employees are not tax-exempt. You are responsible for what is known as FICA. You will have to have employees fill-out a W-4 in order to take out state, federal, and social security. There are a few other taxes from employees' paychecks and it has to be the correct amount or employees will have to pay taxes. You must do your research and stay abreast as tax laws requirements change from time to time. It is to your advantage to hire a bookkeeper, hire an accountant, or a CPA to handle this task. You can have the option of using software that automatically issues payroll checks and make deductions. Or you can rely upon your bank or a company that specialize in offering payroll services. Whatever the case, you must make sure that the taxes arrive on time (quarterly) or you will be hit with a hefty fine.

What are good software systems to use for payroll?
_____

_____

_____

_____

_____

XV. **ADDITIONAL ITEMS**

Below is a list of information to implement in your NFP:

- Policies & Procedures,
- Grievance policy,
- Program record keeping,
- Fiscal record keeping,
- Workman compensation,
- Unemployment insurance,
- Job Titles,
- Job Descriptions,
- Applications,
- Background checks,
- Credit checks,
- Drug tests,
- Resource development,
- Employee evaluations,
- Ordering Equipment & Supplies,
- Staff Development,
- Department of Labor Laws & Wages Assignments, and
- A host of other things.

You are only just beginning.

PURCHASE MY NEXT BOOKs, "Resource Development"

and "For Profit Business" in order to add additional information to your arsenal of running a NFP.

Additional Acknowledgements

I would like to as always acknowledge God my Creator who has guided me through this life of service.

I would like to acknowledge my daughter Rita McClendon, who has been an eye witness of accounts of many trials and triumphs that I have experienced. She has always been by my side.

I would like to acknowledge Patricia Barto who passed many years ago. Oh how I long for her. Patricia connected me to the opportunity to work in a hospital laboratory and en route to become a Medical Laboratory Technician with the designated ASCP recognition in the field of Medical Laboratory Technology.

I will always acknowledge Anna White & Annie Norwood my maternal great-grandmother and grandmother who were very instrumental in my life. My great-grand mother is the person that I acquired organizational skills, the love of travel, and the spirit of an entrepreneurship. Annie my grandmother was instrumental in encouraging me to pursue opportunities. She had a discerning eye. It's because of her that I learned to drive, type, participated in a cotillion, and entered the ministry.

Dr. Eurydice Moore, Business Consultant

Bio Brief

Founder of Eurydice

- Assisted Churches, Schools, and Agencies in acquiring over 3 Million in Resource Development Funding
- An Author of 4 books: Riddy Ann against the ODD, How to set up a Not-for-Profit, A-Z guide in for profit set up, Resource Development a New level of Dimension
- Grew up in Chicago's East-Garfield Community & graduated from Lucy Flower H.S.1974
- Graduated from Central YMCA in A.S degree in Medical Laboratory Technology 1976
- Graduated from College of St. Francis in B.S. degree in Health Arts 1984
- Graduated from Spertus in M.S. in Human Services Administration 1986
- Graduated from Concordia University in M.A. in Urban Education 1993
- Graduated from Northern Illinois's in Advance Certificate in Entrepreneurship Program 1991
- Graduated from Midwest Theological Institute in Indiana in PhD Pastoral Counseling 2004
- Completed City of Chicago's Business Affairs & City College Business Start up 2007
- Completed Mormans Consulting Group's Business Coaching & Business Strategies Trainings 2016
- Medical Laboratory Technician at Rush, Cook County, Mount Sinai, Mary Thompson University of Illinois of Chicago Hospitals 1973-1985
- Educator & Work Study Coordinator at Lucy Flower H.S. 1985-1991
- Guidance Counselor at Morton Career Academy 1991-1995

- Over 30 years of combine Non for Profit experiences at Chicago Public School System, Churches, Social Services Center, Safe Haven Community Skill Center & Hannah Community Development Center 1985-2004
- Established Eurydice Moore & Associates 2004 to presence served over 12,000 clients in distribution of free grant and resource development information, incorporation, and 501(c)(3)
- Established Eurydice January, 2016 to offer business set up, coaching, trainings & development, incorporation, 501(c)(3) set up, grant writing, and resource development.
- Internet & Radio Personality 2005-2007
- CAN TV program in Non for Profit & For Profit Business Resource 2007-2009

Author's Contact Information:

Dr. Eurydice Moore
eurydicemoore1@gmail

Discounted books are available to those who are interested in teaching from this booklet. You may contact me at the above-mentioned email address for discounted books, Consultation Services, Training & Development, and/or Speaking Engagements.

OTHER RESOURCES

LIFE STORY OF THE AUTHOR
THAT LED TO BUSINESS VENTURE

www.ingramcontent.com/pod-product-compliance
Lightning Source LLC
Chambersburg PA
CBHW080414300426
44113CB00015B/2512